AFRICAN ELEPHANTS

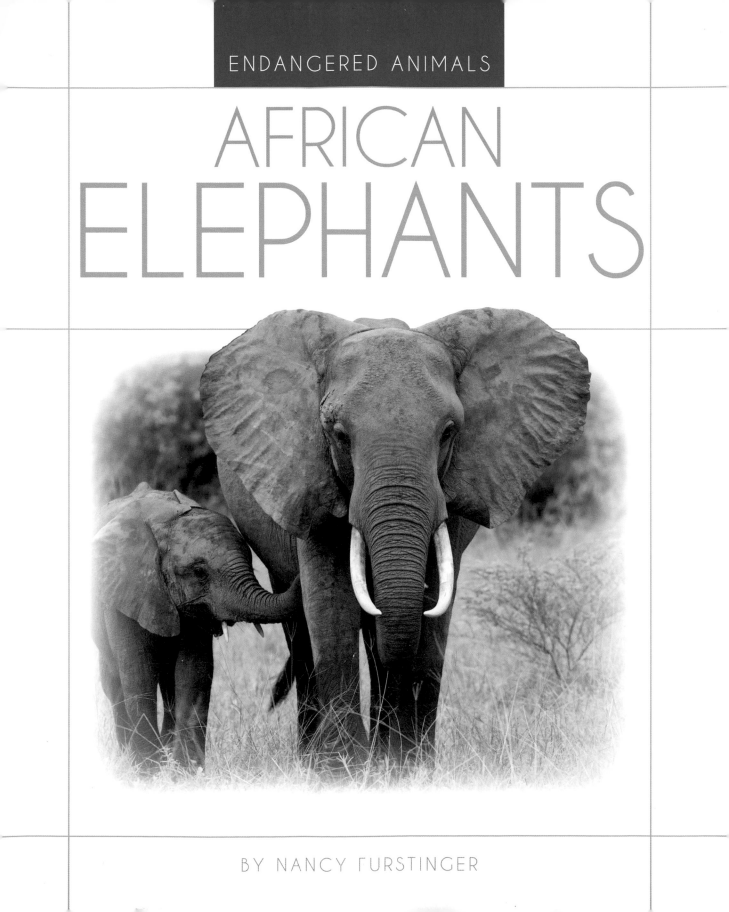

BY NANCY FURSTINGER

Published by The Child's World®
1980 Lookout Drive • Mankato, MN 56003-1705
800-599-READ • www.childsworld.com

Acknowledgments
The Child's World®: Mary Berendes, Publishing Director
Red Line Editorial: Editorial direction and production
The Design Lab: Design
Amnet: Production

Design Element: Shutterstock Images
Photographs ©: Johan W. Elzenga/Shutterstock Images,
cover, 1; Villiers Steyn/Shutterstock Images, 4; Jez Bennett/
Shutterstock Images, 5; Shutterstock Images, 6, 9, 12–13,
22; David De Lossy/Thinkstock, 10; Johan Swanepoel/
Shutterstock Images, 11; Mark Lennihan/AP Images, 16;
Kin Cheung/AP Images, 18–19; Piotr Gatlik/Shutterstock
Images, 21

ISBN 9781631439636
LCCN 2014959634

Printed in the United States of America
Mankato, MN
July, 2015
PA02264

ABOUT THE AUTHOR

Nancy Furstinger has been speaking up for animals since she learned to talk. She is the author of nearly 100 books, including many on her favorite topic: animals! She shares her home with big dogs and house rabbits (all rescued). Furstinger also volunteers for several animal organizations.

TABLE OF CONTENTS

CHAPTER ONE

LAND GIANTS   4

CHAPTER TWO

LOSS OF HABITAT   11

CHAPTER THREE

STRONG LAWS   16

What You Can Do, 22

Glossary, 23

To Learn More, 24

Index, 24

LAND GIANTS

Elephants cool off and suck up a drink at a watering hole.

A herd of elephants visits an African watering hole. The large **mammals** suck water up their long trunks as if they were straws. They roll in the mud to protect their skin from bugs and the hot sun. They flap their big ears like fans to keep cool.

African elephants are the world's largest land animals. There are two types: **savanna** and forest elephants. Adult savanna elephants can be 13 feet (4 m) high at the shoulders. That is about twice the height of a basketball player! Forest elephants are smaller. They can grow up to 8 feet (2.4 m) high. Adult savanna males, called bulls, weigh around 14,000 pounds (6,350 kg). Adult females, or cows, can weigh

At 13 feet tall, elephants have no problem reaching the leaves of a tall tree.

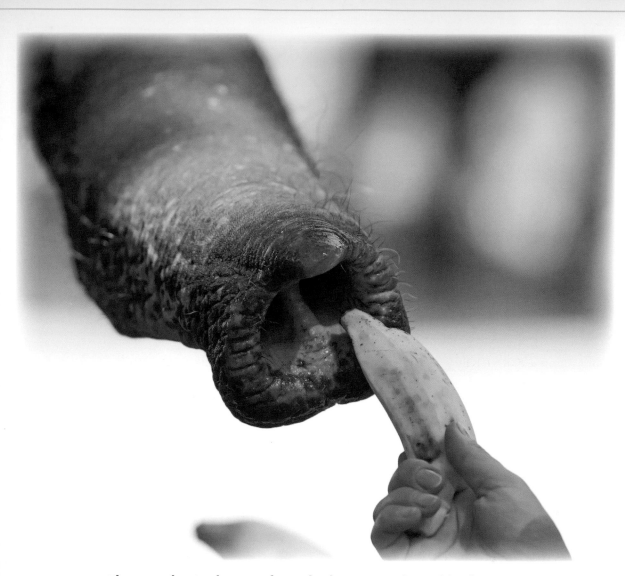

The muscles in the tip of an elephant's trunk act like fingers.

7,000 pounds (3,180 kg). Forest elephants weigh around 6,000 pounds (2,700 kg). The largest African elephant on record weighed 27,000 pounds (12,250 kg). That's equal to the weight of two school buses!

Elephants are covered with wrinkly gray skin. Their large ears can weigh as much as a fifth grader does. An elephant's trunk acts as a nose, a hand, and a tool. Elephants use their trunks to drink, smell, and breathe. Two "fingers" at the tip of their trunks help elephants grab food. There are more than 40,000 muscles in an elephant's trunk. Those muscles make the trunk strong enough to uproot trees.

Both males and females have two tusks. These long, curved teeth are an elephant's **ivory**. Tusks never stop growing. Older bulls can have tusks 8 feet (2.4 m) long. Bulls battle one another using their tusks as weapons. Elephants also use tusks as tools. They dig watering holes, uproot plants, and strip bark from trees.

GOOD VIBRATIONS

To stay safe, elephants give each other signals. They contact others by making a low rumbling sound. Herds can hear this sound up to 6 miles (10 km) away. The sound also travels underground. Elephants feel **vibrations** with their trunks and feet. They can feel the rumbles up to 20 miles (32 km) away.

African elephants can live up to 70 years in the wild. They live in groups called herds. Herds are made up of cows and calves. The oldest and largest cow leads the herd. Mothers, grandmothers, aunts, female cousins, and sisters travel together. Baby elephants grow inside their mothers for nearly two years. A newborn calf can weigh 250 pounds (113 kg). Calves double their weight in their first three months of life. Bull calves leave the herd when they are teenagers. They travel on their own or team up with other bulls.

Herds **migrate** across Africa's vast spaces. Savanna elephants roam savannas, deserts, grassy plains, and woodlands. Forest elephants live in rain forests. Elephants migrate to find food and water and to avoid threats. They spend most of their days searching for food and water. They sleep only a few hours a day. But they spend 16 hours a day eating. Elephants eat grasses, roots, fruit, and bark. Adult elephants eat up to 300 pounds (136 kg) of food each day. They drink up to 30 gallons (114 L) of water each day, too.

Few **predators** attack the large elephants. When in danger, elephants trumpet a low alarm call. This warns their herd of danger. Hyenas and lions might try to attack a calf. The herd will form a circle around the calf to protect it. If elephants need to charge a predator, they can run up to 25 miles per hour (40 kmh).

A baby elephant weighs about as much as a refrigerator.

Humans are the greatest threat to African elephants.

Elephants can protect themselves from wild predators. But they also fight a greater threat: humans. Humans may soon cause elephants to disappear.

CHAPTER TWO

LOSS OF HABITAT

Humans are forcing more elephants onto less land.

In the 1930s and 40s, 4 to 5 million elephants thundered across Africa. But today there are fewer than 500,000. International groups consider African elephants **vulnerable**. The animals will become **endangered** unless people help.

Elephant **habitat** is shrinking. In the past few decades, more people were born in Africa than on any other continent. Today around 1.2 billion people live in Africa. These people need space to live. They clear forests for farms, houses, and roads. They cut down trees for lumber and fuel. Elephants have less land on which to live. More elephants must squeeze into smaller spaces.

Herds of elephants migrate throughout the year. But farmers block many of their routes. They dig canals and put up cattle fences. Some herds try to find other paths. They might move through villages. They knock over huts. Some run over people by accident. Angry farmers poison or shoot the elephants.

Elephants must adapt to the changes people make to their habitat.

Elephants are no match for human hunters. **Poachers** use rifles and other weapons to kill elephants. The poachers are interested in only one thing: ivory tusks. Ivory is valuable. Some call it "white gold." In Asia carved ivory is a sign of wealth. Some people believe tusks fall out like teeth. They do not realize elephants must be killed in order to get tusks.

Poachers target huge bull elephants with tusks weighing more than 100 pounds (45 kg) each. These bulls are called great tuskers. In 2014 an elephant named Satao was poached in Kenya. This great tusker had been the world's largest elephant.

Around 33,000 African elephants are poached every year. Not enough calves are born to replace the killed animals. In 2011 poachers killed one out of every 12 elephants. At this rate, elephants could become **extinct** by the 2030s.

RIGHTIES AND LEFTIES

Elephants use their tusks as tools. An elephant may rely more on either its right or left tusk. This is similar to how humans favor their right or left hands. The favored tusk becomes shorter through wear.

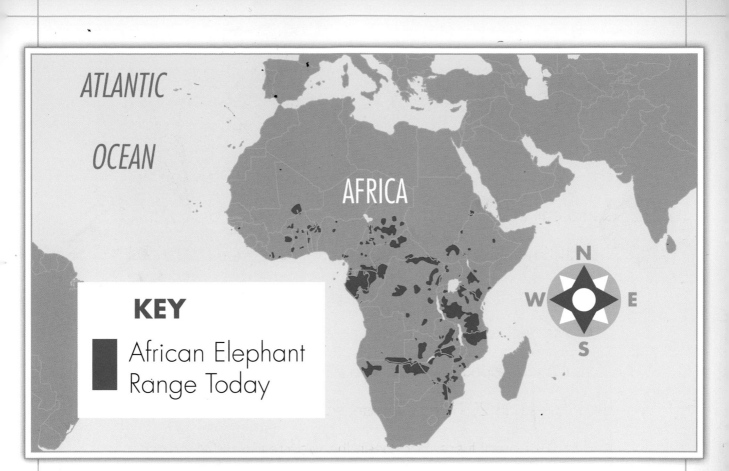

ATLANTIC

OCEAN

AFRICA

KEY

African Elephant
Range Today

**Elephants once roamed across Africa, but
today their range is much smaller.**

Hunting elephants is illegal. However, this does not stop poachers. They can earn more money selling tusks than from farming or herding.

People in Africa and around the world are fighting back. They see the need to protect elephants. People do not want to live in a world without them.

CHAPTER THREE

STRONG LAWS

Elephant ivory can be carved into statues.

In 1990 the sale of ivory was banned around the world. At first, the ban was successful. Many people stopped buying ivory. Shops that carved and sold ivory closed.

Things changed in 1999 and 2008. Some African countries sold ivory to Japan and China. These countries had a supply of ivory collected before the 1990 ban. Ivory was again available to buy. People wanted to buy more ivory. Poachers killed more elephants. They **smuggled** tusks out of Africa.

Now, some countries are taking action. In 2013 the United States government destroyed 6 tons (5 t) of ivory. The governments in China and Hong Kong also destroyed illegal ivory. African countries are also fighting back. In 2014 a new wildlife law passed in Kenya. It strongly punishes people who poach wildlife. The first person punished was a Chinese ivory smuggler. He had to serve seven years in jail or pay $233,000. The tusk he tried to smuggle weighed 7.5 pounds (3.4 kg).

African elephants need to safely roam in the wild. Countries have protected the land where elephants migrate and live. Wildlife groups train guards to protect the elephants. They give the guards tools to watch elephants. They teach guards how to stop poachers. Some groups donate airplanes. A plane can watch elephants from the sky. Elephants can safely move between protected areas. They also move safely between countries in Africa.

Some people help elephants be good neighbors to humans. Scientists tag elephants and track them. People can map where the elephants live and migrate. They build roads, farms, and houses in other places. Some farmers put up electric fences.

This illegal ivory collected in Hong Kong will soon be burned up and destroyed.

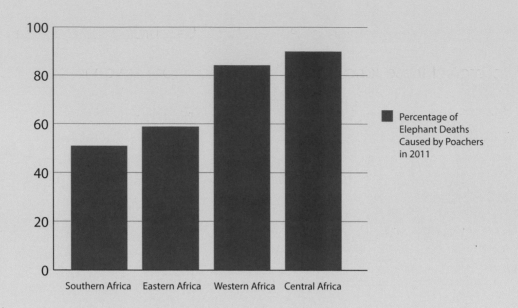

Poachers cause the majority of elephant deaths across Africa.

This keeps elephants away. Others grow hot peppers, which elephants do not like. Farmers make pepper-spray bombs to teach elephants to stay away from crops.

Tourism is another way to save elephants. Tourists pay to travel to national wildlife parks in Africa. People visit Tsavo East National Park in Kenya to shoot big tuskers with cameras, not guns. Guides bring tourists to watch the herds. The tourists' money helps protect parks and wildlife.

Elephants are one of Africa's wild treasures. Humans need to protect these land giants. With help, more savanna and forest elephants will continue to roam the wild.

ELEPHANT NURSERY

A wildlife park in Kenya has rescued more than 150 baby elephants. Some of these orphans lost their families to poachers. Keepers raise the babies. The calves will join wild herds when they are older. Park visitors enjoy watching the babies splash in their daily mud baths.

With help from humans, elephants may once again roam across Africa.

WHAT YOU CAN DO

- Never buy or wear ivory. Instead, choose items made from the nuts of ivory palm trees. These nuts can be carved and polished to look like elephant ivory.

- Your classroom can adopt an African elephant. Hold a fundraiser to raise money for the donation.

- Learn more about elephants by reading books, watching wildlife films, and checking out Web sites. Share what you learn with other students.

GLOSSARY

endangered (en-DANE-jerd) An endangered animal is in danger of becoming extinct. African elephants may become endangered.

extinct (ek-STINKT) If a type of animal is extinct, all the animals have died out. Some scientists believe elephants may become extinct by the 2030s.

habitat (HAB-i-tat) A habitat is a place where an animal lives. Humans destroy elephant habitat.

ivory (EYE-vree) Ivory is the hard, cream-colored substance that forms animal tusks. Poachers hunt elephants for their ivory tusks.

mammals (MAM-alz) Mammals are animals that are warm-blooded, give birth to live young, and are usually covered with hair. African elephants are mammals.

migrate (MYE-grayt) To migrate is to move from one region to another. Elephants migrate to search for water and food.

poachers (PO-churz) Poachers are people who illegally hunt and kill animals. Poachers kill elephants for their tusks.

predators (PRED-a-terz) Predators hunt, kill, and eat other animals. Elephants have few wild predators.

savanna (suh-VAN-uh) A savanna is a flat grassland in a warm region. Some elephants live on the African savanna.

smuggled (SMUH-gulld) If something is smuggled it is moved from one country to another secretly and illegally. Poachers smuggled ivory tusks out of Africa.

tourism (TOOR-iz-um) Tourism is the activity of traveling to a place for pleasure. Tourism may help save elephants.

vibrations (vye-BRAY-shunz) Vibrations are trembling motions. Elephants can feel vibrations through the ground.

vulnerable (VUL-nur-uh-bul) Something that is vulnerable is open to danger or harm. The loss of habitat causes elephants to be considered vulnerable.

TO LEARN MORE

BOOKS

Hall, Kirsten. *African Elephant: The World's Biggest Land Mammal.* New York: Bearport, 2007.

Marsh, Laura. *Great Migrations: Elephants.* Washington DC: National Geographic, 2010.

O'Connell, Caitlin. *A Baby Elephant in the Wild.* New York: Houghton Mifflin Harcourt, 2014.

WEB SITES

Visit our Web site for links about African elephants:
childsworld.com/links

Note to Parents, Teachers, and Librarians: We routinely verify our Web links to make sure they are safe and active sites. So encourage your readers to check them out!

INDEX

behavior, 4, 7, 8
buying and selling of elephant
 ivory, 14, 16–17

calves, 8, 9, 14, 21
China, 17

food, 8
forest elephants, 5, 6, 8, 21

habitat, 8, 11–12
Hong Kong, 17

Japan, 17

Kenya, 14, 17, 20, 21

poachers, 14–15, 17, 18, 21
predators, 9, 10

savanna elephants, 5, 8, 21

tourism, 20
trunks, 4, 7
Tsavo East National Park, 20
tusks, 7, 14, 15, 17

United States, 17